Lands End

To

John O'Groats

GW00775704

900 Miles Through England,

Wales and Scotland

on

The Shortest Cycling Route by Road

Brian Smailes

MILLENNIUM CYCLE RIDES IN 1066 COUNTRY (EAST SUSSEX)
ISBN 1-903568-04-8

Walking Guides   **THE YORKSHIRE DALES TOP TEN**
ISBN 0-9526900-5-5

THE DERBYSHIRE TOP TEN
ISBN 1-903568-03-X

THE COMPLETE ISLE OF WIGHT COASTAL FOOTPATH
ISBN 0-9526900-6-3

ISLE OF WIGHT, NORTH TO SOUTH – EAST TO WEST
ISBN1-903568-07-2

THE NATIONAL 3 PEAKS WALK
ISBN 1-903568-24-2

THE SCOTTISH COAST TO COAST WALK
ISBN 0-9526900-8-X

17 WALKS IN GLEN NEVIS
ISBN1-903568-05-6

THE GREAT GLEN WAY
ISBN 1-903568-13-7

THE YORKSHIRE 3 PEAKS WALK
ISBN 1-903568-22-6

THE LANCASHIRE TRAIL
ISBN 1-903568-10-2

THE LYKE WAKE WALK GUIDE
ISBN 1-903568-14-5

THE 1066 COUNTRY WALK
ISBN 1-903568-00-5

JOHN O'GROATS TO LANDS END
ISBN 1-903568-18-8

SHORT WALKS IN THE LAKE DISTRICT
ISBN 1-903568-20-X

Tourist Guide   **TOURIST GUIDE TO VARADERO, CUBA**
ISBN 1-903568-08-0

LANDS END TO JOHN O'GROATS
(CYCLE GUIDE)
ISBN 1-903568-11-0
FIRST PUBLISHED 2004
CHALLENGE PUBLICATIONS
7, EARLSMERE DRIVE, BARNSLEY. S71 5HH

Brian Smailes

Holds the record for the fastest 4 and 5 continuous crossings of the Lyke Wake Walk over the North York Moors. He completed the 210miles over rough terrain on 5 crossings in June 1995 taking 85hours and 50minutes.

His most recent venture was to walk from John O'Groats to Lands End, completing it in August 2003 in 34 days. In August 2001 he cycled from Lands End to John O'Groats, a journey of over 900miles in 6days 13hours 18minutes. This involved carrying food, clothing and tent, and was completed without support between both ends.

Brian lectures on outdoor pursuit courses and between these travels extensively on walking expeditions and projects around Great Britain.

Long distance running and canoeing are other sports he enjoys, completing 25 marathons and canoeing the Caledonian Canal 3 times.

Having travelled extensively throughout the UK, Europe and the Caribbean, Brian has recently been writing international travel guides to enable the holidaymaker to access the world with ease and enjoy it as much as he does.

CONTENTS

Page

Appendix

PHOTOGRAPHS   **Page**

ACKNOWLEDGEMENTS

In publishing this 1st edition of Lands End to John O'Groats Cycle Guide, I must thank the following people for their help and contribution: -

Pam Smailes and Graham & Sandra Fish for taking me to Lands End.
Pam, David & Madeline Allen for collecting me from John O'Groats.
Elva Hodgson for meeting me halfway.

ISBN 1-903568-11-0
First Published 2004

Published by: -
Challenge Publications, 7 Earlsmere Drive, Barnsley, S71 5HH
Printed by: - Dearne Valley Printers Ltd. Tel: 01709 872188

The information in this book is believed by the author to be correct at publication. No liabilities can be accepted for any inaccuracies, which may be found. Anyone using this book should refer to the relevant map in conjunction with the book and be experienced in map recognition.

The description or representation of a route used does not necessarily mean there is existence of a right of way.

INTRODUCTION

The first 'End to End' was recorded in 1879 by Robert Carlyle, since that time, thousands have completed it in ever increasing numbers. People have attempted this challenge on bicycles, including a penny-farthing bicycle, carried crosses, walked nude, carried doors and bricks, pushed wheelbarrows and travelled by car, wheelchair and aeroplane.

One of the more famous people to complete it is Dr. Barbara Moore in the 1960's. She was probably the person who re-awakened people to the challenge. Also Ian Botham the famous cricketer, his walk was publicised throughout the media and he raised a lot of money for charity.

Lands End to John O'Groats is a minimum of 874miles but as you cannot cycle on motorways then it will be around the 900mile mark. Either way it represents a challenge that cannot be taken lightly. To complete this challenge requires dedication, commitment and a sense of purpose. Training the body and mind to cope with the daily distance is an important aspect in your preparation for this ultimate British challenge.

Lands End is the most southwesterly tip of the English mainland, the central point is the signpost, which points to John O'Groats, New York and The Isles of Scilly. There is a visitor centre with attractions, shops, café and hotel. Lands End itself covers about 100acres and is an area of natural beauty. Many people visit, especially throughout the summer. The sea around Lands End is a graveyard for ships with many wrecks around it, one of the more famous and recent being the Torrey Canyon.

John O'Groats is situated at the northern tip of mainland Scotland with fine views over the Pentland Firth towards the Orkney Islands. Britain's second busiest shipping channel is between these points. There is the last house in Scotland *(photo 7),* a tourist information centre and a cluster of recently built shops. The famous signpost there points to Lands End, near to the start/finish line, where you end your journey.

The name John O'Groats dates back to 1496 when three Dutch brothers, the de Groots, worked on the land and sea in that area. Eventually the area became known as John O'Groats.

The journey between both points is long, can be dangerous on the road, and remote in a number of areas, so correct preparation and planning is essential if you are to complete this cycle route. Follow the advice and recommendations in this book then it is down to you and your ability to stay the course for 900miles.

Between April and October is obviously the best time to attempt this challenge, but the best time would be May/June. This is for a number of reasons: -

A. The days are long and if you are feeling fit, you can make good progress either early morning or late in the evening.

B. It is not usually too hot in May/June compared to July/August and you will not be left feeling exhausted because of the heat and having to drink so much to avoid dehydration.

C. Cycling in May/June means you miss the main holiday time of July/August when B&Bs get booked early and there is a lot more holiday traffic on the roads. Generally it is a lot better to go in May/June.

D. Prices often rise for the main holiday months of July/August in B&Bs and for items in shops, so going earlier means you may not spend as much overall.

JOHN O'GROATS

INVERNESS

STIRLING

CARLISLE

LANCASTER

SHREWSBURY

CHEPSTOW

BRISTOL

TAUNTON

BODMIN

LANDS END

THE CHALLENGE

I have described to you in this book what I feel is the shortest route by road baring a few small exceptions. Generally the route is mostly on 'A' roads but ventures onto some minor roads in Devon and Scotland. The route is the main official challenge route used by most cyclists, and if you take another route then you end up cycling further! It usually takes between 6 and 15 days to complete the journey depending if you are a fast or slow cyclist or if you prefer a more leisurely ride, stopping off in most villages on route.

To cycle between 60 and 120miles a day may seem to some people an easy daily distance, but bear in mind that you do this day in day out and that is the difficult part. Add to this the aching muscles, chafing; numb hands, head on winds and busy traffic, you are in for a hard challenge ahead!

The remoteness of some areas, particularly in Scotland means that it is wise to carry a small supply of food with you. There are shops in some villages but this often means you need to turn off your route to go into the villages, resulting in cycling extra miles and taking longer for your journey overall.

Something that can present a problem is your safety on the road. Wearing something of high visibility is important, as is the wearing of a suitable cycling helmet. These and other safety points will be looked at in detail later.

You can generally divide the route into three sections, Lands End to Bristol, Bristol to Carlisle and Carlisle to John O'Groats. I felt that the hardest section was the last one through Scotland. The more exposed area, the head on winds and the hills to climb can make the trip so much harder. Devon and Cornwall presented a lesser problem, with the many small hills in the area and having to cycle along the A30 in heavy traffic, make it hazardous.

I found it helpful to take a 'bivi' bag or a lightweight tent, which can be used if there are no B&Bs available as can happen. I have included some B&Bs and the Tourist Information Centres on route. This will help you with your planning.

Many people have a support vehicle to accompany them. This is good if you can find someone with the time and vehicle to do it. An estate car where you can sleep in the back is ideal, but any vehicle will do to support you, carry your equipment and supply you with drinks and food on route. On a venture of this type you need to eat regularly, usually little and often to keep your energy levels up.

Now you have an insight into the pleasures and pains on this expedition let us continue our preparation and look at the more detailed planning.

PLANNING PHASE

There are a number of aspects to this section so we will look at each part in detail.

The Route: -

You need to be familiar with the route well before you leave. There are many detailed maps on the market showing the route described in this book. I suggest photocopying only the relevant sections of the route to carry with you. This cuts down on weight and you only have the sections of the route you require with you. The individual sheets can be discarded as you are finished with them.

It is easy planning to cycle a set distance each day, however in practice this can quickly change. You may just be out of energy some days and cannot cycle any further. While taking note where the villages are, cycle as far each day as you feel comfortable with. When I cycled the route, I found it took the first three days to get used to cycling such a long distance each day, after that, some days I could cycle up to 160miles a day; on others it was only 100miles.

The weather can play a big part in how far you can cycle each day. I found that wearing waterproofs was helpful if I was not sweating, but generally I got wetter wearing them, so later in the journey I resorted to only wearing shorts and t-shirt that are quick drying. The rain may have soaked me but it was refreshing and I cycled a lot quicker and further.

One important point is to ensure that the air temperature is warm enough to enable you to wear the minimum of clothing otherwise you may get hypothermia. Smearing Vaseline on the legs and arms will allow the rain to quickly run off and help to keep you warmer. I can recommend this method providing you have dry clothing in your panniers to use if necessary and you are not cold in the rain.

Clothing & Equipment: -

The months before your expedition gives you time to acquire your clothing and equipment. Whatever you buy needs to be strong and durable enough to stand up to the rigours of your expedition. Above all your clothing needs to keep you warm and protected from the elements. Try to purchase light coloured or reflective clothing where possible.

Food: -

Any food you carry should when possible be in small quantities. Throughout the route there are many towns, villages and corner shops to buy food. The areas that are more remote are in Scotland as well as along the A30 in Cornwall. These I have mentioned in other sections of the book.

Carry enough food/snacks for the days when you are cycling in the remote areas. Generally there are fuel stations where you can buy snacks and occasionally you pass truck stops or roadside cafes. These places provide cheap meals and drinks, which I found very welcoming as I progressed along the route.

Try to eat food for energy e.g. fruit, nut type chocolate bars and when stopping for a full meal eat rice, pasta, wholemeal bread or jacket potato. Plan your route to arrive near villages and/or food stops if possible, but have some spare food with you just in case this is difficult.

I did not take a stove with me, due to the space and weight. My main meals were purchased in places like Co-op or Tesco cafés, bar meals and roadside cafes/truck stops.

TRAINING PLAN

To complete a venture like this requires a good level of fitness and stamina. Start your training with short rides and build up over a few months to cycling 90miles a day over a three-day period.

You will find that any extra training you can do in the gym, swimming or jogging will all help, but do not over-do it. Building the leg muscles with a variety of exercises is the important part.

You cannot beat the actual practice on the cycle itself especially with full panniers on. I trained without any extra weight on the cycle and was amazed when I put on the full panniers how hard it was to cycle. This I think is the most important point.

The two weeks before you go ease off on the training and rest more. Use the time to sort out your clothing and equipment. Check the cycle for loose nuts and bolts, handlebars and wheels and ensure you have plenty of high visibility clothing.

SAFETY CONSIDERATIONS

The entire route is on road, which can be extremely busy in parts, especially in rush hour traffic. It is very important to be aware of the hazards a cyclist poses to the unsuspecting driver. Try if possible to make an early start around 5.30am or earlier if you can, depending upon the time of year. This will help you to cover some distance before the traffic builds up on the roads, apart from having cleaner air to breathe.

It is important to wear bright reflective or high visibility clothing, similar to what the police wear. Bright clothing helps you to be seen and could ultimately save your life. I wore bright yellow shorts and vest most of the time in hot weather or when cycling on winding roads.

Take a good lightweight torch, as you may need it during the night or for some other emergency. Do not try to cycle on roads in darkness, as it is very dangerous, use the daylight for cycling. Bicycle safety should still consist of lights front and back as well as a reflector on the back and any other place you can put them. To see is to be seen!

Carry some identity with you and contact friends or relatives regularly to report your position. I found it very helpful to carry a mobile telephone with me. It can be recharged if you stay in a B&B. In some areas there is no reception e.g. mountainous areas and some other places. You can also use your phone if you need to phone a TIC for a B&B or other information.

It is recommended you take a spare inner tube for the cycle as well as a puncture repair kit. If you are unlucky enough to have a puncture, you do not want to be spending a lot of time on a grass verge by a busy road repairing it.

Depending on the time of year you may need midge cream or sun cream. I found these necessary, cycling in August, and especially going through Scotland, as the midges were plentiful and it was hot! A good covering of midge cream and I was thankfully saved from bites. Sunglasses may be of benefit, but that is another item to carry. They did however stop flies getting into my eyes and the wind making them water.

Take plenty of drinks with you and refill where you can, even by knocking on someone's door. If you sweat a lot you may need an extra water bottle. Sometimes it is quite a distance between habitations, particularly in Scotland. Eat little and often during the day to keep your energy levels up, having a good meal in the evening. Carry enough food for the section, and plan ahead but do not take too much as you have to carry it.

Take a good supply of first aid items with you, particularly elastic stockings for leg problems and knee/ankle supports. A tube of anti-histamine cream for nettle or wasp stings is very useful as I found out. A supply of anti-inflammatory tablets can be of use if you are accustomed to swelling of various joints.

Summarising this section, the most important points to consider are the wearing of bright clothing, having plenty of water to avoid dehydration and knee/ankle supports.

YOUR BICYCLE

The cycle you choose is the most important item you take. If you experience problems with your cycle then the whole expedition could be at risk. On an expedition of this length, undertaken in a mixture of weather and usually carrying more weight and equipment than you normally would your cycle is tested to its limits.

There is a wide range of bicycles available for an event of this kind. You do not need to spend hundreds of pounds but spend wisely. The type of cycle most suited to this journey if you are carrying panniers etc is a hybrid type cycle. However if you have support and do not need to carry anything and are looking for a fast journey then a racing cycle will be better suited.

There are numerous events that could affect your journey but below are the things that are most likely to happen to your cycle.

Tyre puncture – Take at least one spare inner tube and a repair kit as well as any spanners etc to remove/tighten vital parts.

Buckled wheel rim – Caused by going over potholes in the road. Ensure the wheels you have on the cycle are of reasonable quality.

Brake blocks wearing down or coming off completely – Start with new blocks and thoroughly check before you leave as there are a lot of hills to descend.

Handlebars getting slack or out of alignment – This can happen with vibration or going over potholes. Ensure the handlebars are fully secured and aligned before you leave.

Panniers or front handlebar bag touching wheels or a moving part – Although they may seem a good fit initially, once you fill them, the weight and movement can often dislodge them and this can ultimately delay you on your journey.

Chain coming off or breaking – This can happen if the chain is too slack, too tight or not lubricated. Ensure the chain is fitted properly and have a trial run before leaving to see if it is fitted correctly. If unsure, visit a cycle shop to have it checked. Keep the chain links thoroughly lubricated.

Lights – Although it is not advisable to cycle at night, you should still have lights that operate. Insert new batteries before you start and ensure lights operate correctly.

Slack wheels – If not secured well before you leave, then again the potholes will loosen them and you may fall off!

From all the above points, the cycle shops tell me that buckled wheel rims are the main problem due to inferior metal and rims. As far as quality is concerned, you get what you pay for.

Other important considerations are: -

1. Cycle clips if you have trousers that could get caught in the chain.
2. A cycle helmet is essential for safety.
3. A cycle raincoat/cape is essential to protect you from the elements.
4. Gel gloves are essential if you don't want numb hands because of the constant pressure on the nerves of the hands pressing on the handlebars.
5. A clear waterproof plastic pocket that sits on the handlebars or on the front carrying bag is helpful so you can put map or route description in.
6. Reflective/high visibility jacket/shorts, stripes on other items. Be safe be seen. *(Photo 8)*

PUBLICITY & SPONSORSHIP

With events of this kind it is not just the challenge of completing the journey but to raise sponsorship for a worthwhile cause. There are many charities that will produce sponsorship forms for you to circulate among family/friends etc. This can sometimes bring in thousands of pounds for the charity of your choice.

An alternative to the traditional way of sponsorship is guessing your finishing time. You could charge people for guessing when you will finish in days, hours, minutes and seconds from the start line to the finish line. It is of course pure guesswork.

Asking companies for donations is worth considering especially if you are having a support vehicle and you are prepared to advertise their company on the vehicle. They may even buy your equipment for you, provide the vehicle, or fuel for the journey.

Publicity in your local area will help with sponsorship. Any unusual method of travelling between the two points may warrant publicity in national magazines or on TV. Local radio stations can be contacted to give live interviews, but set this up before you leave home.

You may find you can get support bandages etc or other items you may be likely to use sponsored by chemist shops or companies.

When I cycled I put on a t-shirt with Lands End to John O'Groats on it. I was amazed how generous people were with donations, free tea and food etc., particularly at roadside mobile cafes. If you can also put the name of a national charity on the same t-shirt then you should do even better in raising money for your charity.

One final word on sponsorship/publicity, you can be as successful as your imagination and determination will allow you. Think about how much you want to raise and what clothing, equipment or fuel you can get sponsored, then set about your task with enthusiasm.

FINANCIAL CONSIDERATIONS

A challenge such as this can make a sizeable hole in your pocket if you do not plan it properly. Initially you need to purchase your main equipment, bicycle, trainers, panniers, tent and clothing if you do not already have them. You may be able to get them sponsored either by a local shop or business or from a national supplier. This may however be difficult as national suppliers get hundreds of letters asking for equipment, so unless you can offer something different on your cycle ride, then there is often not much chance of getting anything from them.

Once you have your equipment you need to plan how to get to Lands End. Haulage Company's have a network of contacts and may be able to help, so make enquiries early. There are train services to Penzance and you are able to take a cycle on them, again enquire early. You then need to cycle the 12miles to Lands End to start your expedition. On reaching John O'Groats, you have to cycle back 17miles to Wick, where you can get a train to other parts of the UK.

Assuming you are travelling without support, your biggest cost will be B&Bs or camping, along with food. B&Bs can be as much as £35.00 in some places, especially in the south and £15.00 near John O'Groats but generally prices were around the £20.00 - £25.00 mark. I recommend carrying a small lightweight tent or a bivi bag. There are places where there are no B&Bs on route or they may be full and you may need to sleep outdoors as I did some nights.

You can always cycle shorter distances each day and fit your schedule to where the villages are. Advantage is that you will have a good bed and shower at night, but the disadvantage is that you will often have to cycle generally 2 - 4miles into a village to find one, and then back the next day to the main route. This will increase and prolong your overall journey. The other disadvantages of staying in a B&B are that you will probably get a late start each morning and of course the cost of staying there compared to camping. It is worth considering using B&Bs one night and camping the next.

When I cycled, I stayed on the main route all the time but noted where the villages were that I would pass through and I tried to ensure I reached a B&B before nightfall. Sometimes there were no B&Bs around at all and others were full so I used my small tent in a nearby field. It is important to carry at least a 'bivi' bag for emergency, but you may prefer to take a small tent and camp more often.

Should you have a support team then the costs involved with that can be substantial. I travelled without support until the final 40miles of the expedition. This is not a problem as long as you can wash your clothes and get them dried. I attached mine to the straps on my cycle to dry, which was very effective.

The above is a resume of the main financial considerations but work your own costs out giving consideration to the above points.

THE START/FINISH

Beside the entrance to the Lands End complex is a start/finish line, and there is a similar line at John O'Groats outside the hotel.

You could not leave Lands End without a photograph at the signpost to record your start and equally at the signpost at John O'Groats to record your finish.

Lands End is a tourist attraction and has many visitors. If you have a support vehicle with you, entry to the car park is free if they mention to the attendant they are doing support. Inside the complex you can purchase food and drinks as well as view the attractions, which are free to 'End to Enders' starting or finishing there.

You will see the start line ahead as you reach the main building. **Go to the post room, just inside the 'Miles of Memories' attraction on the right as you enter, to collect your form and have it stamped. If arriving at night, go to the hotel reception nearby.**

Arriving in John O'Groats, you have a beautiful view of the nearby islands *(photo 7)*. The air is clean and fresh usually with a slight wind blowing most of the time. There is a tourist information centre and a café as well as a collection of small gift shops. The hotel on the front has been closed for a number of years and awaiting refurbishment although the bar on the ground floor is open.

The passenger ferry leaves from the small harbour nearby stopping off at the islands. **The last house in Scotland is nearby the harbour** *(photo 7)*. **In here you have your form stamped to complete your expedition.** Should the shop be closed then you can go to the bar in the hotel a short distance away.

The form should be stamped where possible on route to show that you stopped at places on your journey. Some receipts should be kept for B&Bs or from shops showing dates, places etc, and handed in at John O'Groats for verification if needed.

Try to finish during normal daytime hours as transport back to Wick is daytime only and the café and shops are closed in the evenings.

PRACTICAL ADVICE

- Ensure you can understand and read a map well enough before you start.

- Ensure the maps used are up to date showing current roads.

- Try to plan your night stops to coincide with the B&Bs shown in this book or at villages.

- Plan a training programme; gradually increase distance and body strength.

- Ensure clothing is bright or has reflective stripes on it.

- Ensure you wear a cycle helmet.

- Ensure all food, clothing and other items carried are kept to a minimum.

- If possible, have someone to meet you on your journey with a change of clothing to save washing.

- Use every opportunity to replenish food and drink stocks.

- Eat little and often and drink plenty throughout the day.

- Alternate between B&Bs and bivi bag/tent if possible for a bath one day and an early start the next.

- Be aware of traffic at all times in front and from behind.

- Keep details on your person of next of kin, medical information, blood group etc. in case of accident.

THE ROUTE

The route is generally well signposted throughout so you should not have much problem. I would advise you to have a list of the relevant road numbers in front of you on your cycle handlebars so you can check without having to take out your map each time you want to check a route.

In the route described below, I will not mention every twist and turn but concentrate on the road numbers, as these are mostly signposted. I will mention notable points on some parts of the route to help guide you through those parts. This route section is also abbreviated to cut out irrelevant words and the text has been enlarged so you can read it from a distance on the cycle.

1. Starting on the start line outside the Lands End main building, cycle along the road *(photo 1)* passing through a number of small villages on the winding, undulating A30 road. Keep on main road to descend a hill after 12miles, arriving at the Tesco roundabout on outskirts of Penzance.

2. Next section approx. 6miles to Hale roundabout still on A30 with both 2-way and dual carriageway right to the far side of Bodmin. Cross a number of roundabouts with St. Michael's Mount off to your right *(photo 2).* Continue on same road passing Cambourne and monuments on hillside off to your right.

3. Continue towards Bodmin passing Blackwater then Indian Queens, still on a 2-way section of A30. Approaching Bodmin, cycle a further 26miles by-passing Bodmin then passing the turning to Jamaica Inn before arriving at Launceston outskirts on A30.

4. Stay on A30, now dual carriageway, to B3260 turn off to Okehampton centre. The road is not so busy now as you pass through the high street in Okehampton. At far side of town, turn left onto the B3215 towards Crediton for approx. 5miles before leading onto the A3072 then onto the A377 taking you into Crediton.

5. The road between Crediton and Tiverton is very undulating. Follow signs to Tiverton on the A3072 then A396, turning right to avoid town centre. Pass over a series of roundabouts taking you to A361 dual carriageway. Cycle on this road for 7miles to J27 of the M5.

6. A 'Little Chef' is nearby as you now cycle on the A38 2-way road initially ascending from the roundabout then on to the village of Wellington. You now have a 5mile stretch to Taunton. On entering, follow the one-way system to the far side of the town then at a large roundabout, follow A38 signs towards North Petherton and Bridgwater, turning left at lights on dual carriageway to cross the canal.

7. This section is reasonably flat as you pass through North Petherton then into Bridgwater. Stay on A38 following signs for Highbridge then pass through a series of small villages, follow signs for Bristol or airport. Pass Bristol Airport on the undulating road and descend gradually into Bristol on A38.

8. Follow signs towards city centre then as you cross the river Avon, turn left onto the A4 going under the Clifton Suspension bridge towards Avonmouth 5miles ahead. Stay on A4 going under the M5 to the large roundabout at Avonmouth then onto A403 towards the Severn Bridge *(2nd crossing, photo 3).*

9. Pass the 1st Severn Crossing then just before reaching the motorway over the 2nd Severn Bridge, turn left on a minor road then right, taking you past the bridge maintenance depot on a cycle path to emerge on the cycle track on the left side of the bridge *(photo 3).* Cyclists can cross free so continue to the far side then descend a path on the left, turning right under the motorway then left up a cycle track, now on the right side.

10. Ascend to the roundabout following signs A48 Chepstow then A466 to Monmouth. Pass Chepstow racecourse and continue on winding road passing Tintern Abbey and Llandogo before reaching Monmouth. Cross the A40 into Monmouth and follow the road through town on the A466 towards Hereford.

11. Stay on A466 then when it merges with A49, turn left cycling into Hereford. Cross main bridge in Hereford then follow signs, right at the roundabout then further on turning left still on the A49 towards Leominster *(photo 4)*. 6miles north of Hereford is a steep ascent to Queenswood Country Park on top of the hill but with a steep descent on far side. Approaching Leominster, stay on by-pass still on A49 to Ludlow.

12. Approaching Ludlow, turn left on the minor road into Ludlow, go directly through town to rejoin A49 on north side. Continue on A49 past Craven Arms and Church Stretton until you reach the ring road around Shrewsbury. Cross ring road cycling straight through town following signs A49 Whitchurch. Stay on A49 to Whitchurch and on meeting the ring road, continue as before directly through town centre. Rejoin A49 on north side again.

13. Next part is through a flatter area but with few facilities until Warrington. Stay on A49, passing Weaverham then cross M56 before arriving at Stockton Heath then into Warrington. Just before the town centre in Warrington, cross a large bridge then at the large roundabout there, which is usually very busy, turn right following signs for Newton Le Willows and M62.

14. At the M62, cross over it still on A49 and cycle directly to Newton Le Willows then Ashton–in-Mackerfield. Continue to Wigan on A49 and stay on this road through Standish and Coppull. You should see M6 off to your left as you reach Charnock Richard. Follow signs now for Euxton and Preston, staying on A49 until you see signs for A6 into Preston.

15. Cycle along a stretch of dual carriageway as you enter Preston. The road ascends passing the park on your right still on the A6. The road now is flat for around 30miles leaving Preston, going under the M55 and heading for Garstang on A6. Turn off to Garstang; it is shorter and quicker to head into Garstang and through to far side, picking up the A6 again.

16. You now have a 12mile section into Lancaster. At the roundabout as you enter Lancaster, follow the one-way system round the city, crossing the river bridge and staying on A6 to Carnforth. Again, stay on A6 following signs for Hale, Milnthorpe or Kendal. You emerge on the A590 dual carriageway and turn right then after a short distance left on A591 taking you to Kendal.

17. After 3miles, bear right onto the A6 directly into Kendal. Cycle through the high street and stay on A6 following signs for Shap and Penrith. Once you leave Kendal there is a gradual ascent to the top of Shap Fell. It can be a very inhospitable area in adverse weather conditions, so be well prepared and ensure you have spare clothing and food with you. After crossing the summit, there is a long descent on the far side still on A6 taking you into Shap Village where there is a small supermarket and post office.

18. From Shap, continue on the undulating A6 road passing Hackthorpe and Lowther then eventually emerging at the roundabout on A66 just before Penrith. Cross with care, cycling into Penrith centre and stay on A6 following signs for Plumpton and Carlisle. This is a quiet undulating road where you can make good progress to Carlisle.

19. Arriving at the roundabout at M6, continue on same road into Carlisle centre. Follow the one-way system and signs for Gretna or Dumfries A7, A74 or A75. You come to a roundabout at far side of City then cross the bridge. Cycle a further 2miles on A7 to another roundabout that takes you to the end of M6 and start of A74 and go across the M6 and down the slip road onto A74 heading north.

20. This dual carriageway is approx. 4miles and is extremely busy, and is the main border crossing into Scotland. Cycle along here to the turn off to Gretna, which is also the start of the A74M. Turn off the slip road into Gretna following into Gretna Green. Look for cycle signs and pick up the B7076 to Kirkpatrick Fleming.

21. You are now on a quiet road with long stretches, running right up to Crawford, parallel with the A74M motorway. There are some small villages but very few shops. Continue on through Kirtlebridge then Ecclefechan on B7076. When you reach the roundabout near Lockerbie, you can either continue north or cycle the short distance into Lockerbie where there are cafes and a variety of shops.

22. Continuing from Lockerbie, stay on this somewhat isolated road with few amenities and pass Beatock. Cycle into Crawford where there is limited accommodation. A short distance on is Abington where there is a shop. Cycle through, then at the roundabout at far side, turn right following signs for Roberton and Lanark A73. Pass through Roberton staying on A73.

23. Continue through Lanark town centre where there are many shops and stay on A73 through to Carluke then outskirts of Wishaw, passing over a number of roundabouts in between. The next 4miles on A73 takes you to Chapelhall as you pass over the M8. A further 3miles takes you into

Important Road Update

The section of dual carriageway between Carlisle & Gretna has recently been improved to motorway standard. It is due to open in December 2008. This means that cyclists cannot ride on the motorway, but should be able to use the new service road, that I am advised, runs parallel with the motorway.

Please check maps and road details for this short section before leaving.

Photo 1
Leaving Lands End, the long road ahead

Photo 2
Leaving Penzance with view of St. Michaels Mount.

24. The B8011 crosses the A80 dual carriageway onto the B816 to Castlecary. Once through the village, turn onto the A80 for ½mile to the start of the M80 then off onto the A803 following signs for Denny and Stirling. The road runs parallel with M80 as you cycle through this built up area of Denny then Dunipace on the A872. After cycling through a section of agricultural land, you cross over the M9, follow signs for Bannockburn and St. Ninians now joining the A9 and passing Bannockburn Visitors Centre on your left.

25. Continue into Stirling centre and cross a bridge over the river following signs to Bridge of Allan. You pass near Wallace monument as you cycle through a shopping area leaving Stirling, then cross a bridge into Bridge of Allan. Stay on A9 to Dunblane 3miles further and pass through the town to join the B8033 for ¾mile to the A9 dual carriageway. Turn right here onto the A9 for 3½miles to the turn off to Greenloaning on the A822.

26. Stay on this road for approx. 12miles passing through Braco then Muthill on this sometimes hilly, winding, isolated road to Crieff. In Crieff there are shops and many B&Bs. Cycle up the hill in town, then turn right into the main high street. Continue through on the A85 following Perth signs then turn left following signs for Aberfeldy on A822. This winding, undulating and isolated road stretches 14miles and passes through Amulree before a turn left onto A826 into Aberfeldy, a further 9miles.

27. There are shops in Aberfeldy before you cycle into the more remote region of the highlands. In the town centre follow signs for Weem and Tummel Bridge and cross the humpback bridge over the river onto the B846 minor road. Cycle this isolated road into Tummel Bridge passing occasional houses on route. Entering Tummel Bridge, the power station is on left with good views over the river area opposite.

28. Stay on the B846 bearing left towards Kinloch Rannoch then after approx. ½mile, turn right onto a very minor road which ascends for approx. 3miles by a forest to emerge near Trinafour. Turn right into Trinafour then left in the village towards the A9 at Dalnacardoch. This is on a one-track road over the open moor. You emerge on the busy A9 where you turn left.

29. The road now has a cycle-way intermittently along the A9 for a considerable distance. Cycle on the cycle-way where possible, or on the A9 where necessary, right to Inverness and beyond for over 100miles. The wind can be strong along the A9 as you pass over Drumochter summit then further on passing turn off for Dalwhinnie. Further ahead pass turn off for Newtonmore and Kingussie, cycling towards Aviemore through some spectacular scenery.

Photo 3
Looking across the Severn Bridge.
The cycle track is on the left side of the bridge.

Photo 4
A last look back at Hereford

30. Pass the turning into Aviemore, unless you need food or accommodation, and continue on A9 passing over Slochd summit then past Tomatin and the Little Chef Services there (a good stopping off place). Ascending gently towards the hills overlooking Inverness on A9, you come to Daviot Village then soon after a tourist information on your left. From here it is downhill to Inverness and the main bridge over the Moray Firth.

31. Inverness has many B&Bs and shops 1½miles off to the left at the bridge, otherwise pass the football stadium on your right and cross the impressive bridge ahead *(photo 5),* still on A9. You are now on the Black Isle heading for Tore roundabout approx. 7miles ahead along this busy dual carriageway. If you turn left just across the bridge into North Kessock and cycle to the bottom of the road, there is a small supermarket on the left where you can purchase food etc.

32. Arriving at the Tore roundabout continue on the A9 towards Alness and Tain. After approx. 7miles, cross the long bridge off the Black Isle and turn right at roundabout on the north side of the Cromarty Firth to eventually by-pass Alness. Continue on A9 to by-pass Tain unless stopping for food or B&B. On outskirts of Tain on A9 is the Glenmorangie distillery on the right, which is a good place to stop for a visit.

33. Descend the hill past the distillery to the roundabout beside the bridge crossing Dornoch Firth. Cross the long bridge still on A9 to by-pass Dornoch on route to Golspie, 6½miles further. Cross another shorter bridge before cycling a further 5miles into Golspie. There are some shops here in the main street. You have now reached the final leg of your expedition. Leaving Golspie, you pass Dunrobin Castle on your right and continue to Brora where there are also shops and other amenities.

34. Cycle the long straight street through the town then through the villages of Loth and Portgower on this 21mile section, descending the hill into Helmsdale. There are some shops there just off the main through road. Now you ascend the long winding road out of County of Sutherland. Next section is extremely hilly *(photo 6)* as you proceed on the winding road to Berriedale and the steepest hill on the journey.

35. Descend with care then ascend winding road on far side. Further on you again come to a steep descent and ascent at Dunbeath. After this place, the remainder is generally flatter as you cycle to Latheron Wheel where there is a butchers and sweet shop on right just off the main road. At Latheron Village, leave the A9 and cycle by the coast on the A99 through a series of very small villages, Lybster, Occumster, Ulbster then Thrumster.

Photo 5
The outskirts of Inverness and the first sign for John O'Groats.

Photo 6
One of the steep descents and ascents between Helmsdale and Dunbeath.

36. Arriving in Wick, cycle straight through, crossing the bridge in the centre and out at the far side passing Caithness Glass factory. Continuing on through the villages of Reiss, Keiss, Auckengill and Freswick, stay on A99 following signs to John O'Groats. You ascend a hillside before descending into John O'Groats.

37. Passing the Seaview Hotel, cycle to the harbour and cross the finish line beside the John O'Groats Hotel. Look for the last house in Scotland *(photo 7)*, where you register your journey. If the shop is closed, go to the John O'Groats Hotel to register there. Do not forget the photo at the signpost *(photo 8)*.

Congratulations on completing
Lands End to John O'Groats.

CONCISE ROUTE SUMMARY

Lands End – A30
Penzance – A30
Bypass Cambourne – A30
Bypass Bodmin – A30
Launceston – B3260/A30
Okehampton – A3072/B3215
Crediton – A396/A3072
Tiverton – A38/A361
Taunton – A38
Bridgwater – A38
Bristol Airport – A38
Under Clifton Suspension Bridge – A4
Exit from Bristol – A4
Avonmouth – A403
Severn Bridge – cycle path on left side
Chepstow – A466
Monmouth – A49/A466
Hereford Town Centre – A49
Bypass Leominster – A49
Ludlow Town Centre – A49 – minor road
Craven Arms – A49
Church Stretton – A49
Shrewsbury Town Centre – A49
Whitchurch – A49
Weaverham – A49
Warrington – A49
Newton le Willows – A49
Ashton in- Makerfield – A49
Wigan – A49
Standish – A49
Bypass Leyland – A6/A49
Preston – A6
Garstang Village – A6/B6430
Lancaster – A6
Carnforth – A6
Kendal – A6
Shap – A6
Penrith – A6
Carlisle – A74
Gretna Green – B7076
Bypass Lockerbie – B7076
Bypass Moffat – B7076
Abington – A702
Roberton – A73
Lanark – A73
Carluke – A73

Chapelhall – A73
Airdrie – A73
Luggiebank – B8039
Cumbernauld Village – A8011
Castlecary – A9
Denny – A872
Dunipace – A872
Bannockburn – A9
Stirling – A9
Bridge of Allan – A9
Dunblane – A9
Greenloaning – A822
Muthill – A822
Crieff – A822
Amulree – A826
Aberfeldy – B846
Coshieville – B846
Tummel Bridge – minor road
Trinafour – minor road
Pass of Drumochter – A9
Dalnaspidal – A9
Bypass Dalwhinnie – A9
Bypass Kingussie – A9
Bypass Aviemore – A9
Slochd Summit – A9
Daviot – A9
Bypass Inverness – A9
North Kessock – A9
Tore roundabout – A9
Alness – A9
Tain – A9
Bypass Dornoch – A9
Golspie – A9
Brora – A9
Helmsdale – A9
Dunbeath – A9
Latheron – A9
Lybster – A99
Occumster – A99
Ulbster – A99
Thrumster – A99
Wick – A99
Keiss – A99
Auckengill – A99
Freswick – A99
John O'Groats – A99

Photo 7
The last house in Scotland where you register your finish.
John O'Groats Hotel is on your left

39

Photo 8
A night time finish at John O'Groats
and the customary photograph.
Note the reflective jacket and strips on wheels.

SUPPORT TEAM

Many people attempt this expedition each year; some have full support, some partial support, and others have none. Finding someone who has the time to spare to accompany you can be a problem, but if you can find someone it can make life a lot easier. Disadvantages are the time element, the cost of accommodation and fuel for the vehicle. Advantages are that you can stop when you have had enough and be picked up as well as receive regular drinks and food on route. Best vehicles for support are a van or an estate car, which you can sleep in each night, so choose wisely.

Mobile telephones are helpful for both the support and yourself so you can keep in contact. It is easy to miss each other, especially when going through large towns or encountering vehicle one-way systems.

Alternatively a supporter who can meet you once or twice on your journey with clean clothing and food etc. is helpful, but if you have support for the whole journey then you need to ask yourself the following questions: -

1. How many people do you need to give adequate support? More people, more cost, more food, more sleeping provision.

2. What sleeping arrangements have you for the support team, camping, B&B or in the back of a van or estate car for the night?

3. Is the vehicle roadworthy and is it a thirsty one?

4. Have you enough room in the vehicle for all clothing and equipment and is there room if you are sleeping in it.

5. Are the support team or person equipped and trained to cope with map reading and first aid as well as long days driving?

6. What facilities have you for washing/drying of everyone's clothes?

QUESTIONS YOU MAY ASK

How long will it take to cycle and how many miles is it?
The distance is approximately 900miles, some say 910 –
960miles but as far as I know, the shortest distance is
874miles on motorways etc. Allowing for the by-roads
and winding minor roads it is at least 900miles.

It will normally take between 6 - 15 days but it depends if
you cycle into villages off route for accommodation and
the weather, muscle/hand problems, weight of cycle overall including panniers, any support and speed to name but
a few. If you do it in less time then you are fit!

Are there any areas I can get lost on?
Generally the route is well signposted and if you take the
route sections of map and a copy of the route described in
this book then you should not have a problem. You do not
need a compass. Look for the road numbers and places, if
you are not sure then ask.

Is the route safe?
I found the route generally safe apart from the busy roads
and the winding country lanes where you have to take
extra care and try to always wear some high visibility
clothing. As regards general safety, the route is no problem but always be cautious. I never had any problems on
my expedition anywhere.

**Which were the areas that presented most problems
when cycling?**
The main problems I encountered were not seeing any
shops where I could buy food, drinks or other items.
There was not even a pub where I could obtain a meal.
This was mainly from Aberfeldy up to Inverness, and
along the A9 road. The section from Gretna Green to
Lanark was also short of shops, as was the A30 from
Penzance to Okehampton.

The other area that presented problems was around Tiverton and Crediton in Devon because of the short undulating hills. Just before Queenswood Country Park near Hereford there is a long steep ascent and there is also the daunting Shap Fell to climb between Penrith and Kendal. Around Berriedale and generally through north-east Scotland there are many steep and undulating roads.

Are there plenty B&Bs on route?

No, there are not many throughout the route. When starting, there are plenty in Penzance area and again in John O'Groats and Wick when finishing and generally in most villages through Scotland. There are few B&Bs between Wishaw and Stirling. Along the A9 there are few B&Bs unless you turn into a village.

Depending on the time of year you may find the B&Bs are full, especially in July/August. Cycling along the A30 in Cornwall there was none so either be prepared to go into a village nearby or to wild camp in a field just off the road. Between Whitchurch and Preston there was only one that I saw and between Crawford and Gretna there are only two or three B&Bs. New B&Bs open as do others close, so you may come across others on your journey.

The alternative is to telephone the TIC's (see appendix) throughout the route to obtain current B&B lists and pre-book all the way. The danger in doing this is that it is a long way and anything can happen with injuries, tiredness, punctures, mechanical failure, the weather and overall fitness that may slow you down and prevent you from reaching the B&B you pre-booked.

I tried to plan to be near a village on route in the evening but it did not always work out and if there are no B&Bs for 60miles then you have no option but to sleep outside or cycle off route into a village.

What should I take in terms of clothing/equipment?

The following list may help you, but each person has different requirements. **Remember when packing your cycle bags/panniers that ounces turn into pounds so choose carefully: -**

1 tracksuit
Lightweight tent or bivi bag
3 pairs of shorts (high visibility)
3 tops (1 long sleeve, 2 t-shirts) high visibility
Water bottles (2 recommended)
Small multiple use army knife
Mobile telephone
Elastic bandages/knee supports etc.
Sun cream/midge cream/sting relief
Travel Wash (for washing clothing)
Survival bag/whistle
Food/sweets/fruit
Spanners
Tube Repair Kit
Cagoul/overtrousers

Personal items
Toilet paper
Notepaper/pencil
Torch (small)
4 pairs of socks
Camera
First aid kit
Cap/woolly hat
Trainers
Toiletries etc.
Sleeping Bag
Spare inner tube
Cycle lights
Cycle helmet
Gel gloves

Is the whole route on road and are there any cycle lanes?

Yes, it is the shortest route by road with only two small exceptions, to avoid long steep hills or winding dangerous bends. There are cycle lanes intermittently on roads throughout the route but the main cycle tracks are on the A9 heading to Inverness where you can, in parts, be totally off the main road but cycling close by it. At no point on the route do you cycle on motorways.

How much of the route is dual carriageway and how much two-way road?

There are sections of dual carriageway intermittently from Penzance to Okehampton and shorter sections throughout the route. In Scotland there are longer stretches of dual carriageway on the A9.

What is the general state of the roads for cycling on?

The roads throughout are good but on any road you will always come across the occasional pothole or severely worn section of road.

FIRST AID

Should you be unfortunate to sustain an injury then it would be helpful if you have knowledge of basic first aid and a first aid kit with you.

Common Types of Injuries

Cuts and grazes	*Frozen Hands*	*Blisters*
Hypothermia	*Sprained Ankle/Wrist*	*Gashed Shins*
Shin Splints	*Bee/Nettle Stings*	*Midge bites*

Individual First Aid Kit

Adhesive Dressing	*Blister Treatments*	*Scissors*
Triangular Bandage	*Crepe Bandage*	*Micropore*
Sterile Dressing	*Safety Pins*	*Insect Repellent*
Bandage	*Gauze/Lint*	*Sun Cream*

Hypothermia

If not prepared for the conditions or your clothing is not satisfactory, a combination of cold, wet, exhaustion and wind chill factor can cause the body core temperature to fall below 35°C resulting in hypothermia.

Ways of Preventing Hypothermia

1. Build up body clothing in thin layers, adding on or taking off as necessary.
2. Have suitable wind/waterproofs with you.
3. Eat some food/hot drink or boiled sweets, which produce energy and heat during digestion.
4. Wear a hat to insulate the head, and some gloves.
5. Take a survival bag for emergencies and if conditions dictate, use it.

APPENDIX

Tourist Information Centres on Route

Penzance	01736 362207
Bodmin	01208 76616
Launceston	01566 772321
Okehampton	01837 53020
Crediton	01363 772006
Tiverton	01884 255827
Taunton	01823 336344
Bridgwater	01278 427652
Bristol	0906 7112191
Chepstow	01291 623772
Monmouth	01600 713899
Hereford	01432 268430
Leominster	01568 616460
Ludlow	01584 875053
Shrewsbury	01743 350761
Whitchurch	01948 664577
Warrington	01925 632571
Wigan	01942 825677
Preston	01772 253731
Kendal	01539 725758
Penrith	01768 867466
Carlisle	01228 625600
Gretna Green	01461 337834
Moffat	01683 220620
Lanark	01555 661661
Stirling	01786 475019
Crieff	01764 652578
Aberfeldy	01887 820276
Kingussie	01540 661297
Aviemore	01479 810363
Daviot Wood	01463 772203
Inverness	01463 234353
Dornoch	01862 810400
Wick	01955 602596
John O'Groats	01955 611373

Distances between Towns/Villages

To find a distance, read down then right. e.g. Berriedale to Dunbeath = 6.9miles

Lands End
⇩

Penzance ➡	12
Hayle (A30)	8
Redruth (A30)	9.4
Victoria	24.9
Bodmin	8.6
Okehampton	42
Crediton	21

⇩

Tiverton ➡	14.4
North Petherton	30.9
Cross village	20.6
Bristol Airport	11.8
Severn Bridge (south east)	20.6
Tintern Abbey	8.7
Monmouth	13.5
Hereford	20.9
Leominster	14.7
Dorrington	33.4
Shrewsbury	7.5
Whitchurch	22.3
Stockton Heath	36.4
Warrington	4.3
Wigan	12.6
Standish Village	4.1
Euxton	9
Preston	8.1
Barton	5.6
Lancaster	20.8
Carnforth	7
Kendal	12.8
Shap	17.7
Hackthorpe	5.8
Carlisle Centre	26.6

Longtown	9.8
Gretna	3.7
Kirkpatrick Fleming	4.6
Ecclefechan	7.5
Crawford	43.2
Abington	3.6
Lanark	19.3
Carluke	5.9
Airdrie	13.8
Cumbernauld	6.6
Dunblane (south)	23.4
Braco	9.8
Crieff	10.8
Amulree	12.5
Trinafour	30.2
Drumochter Summit	14.3
Dalwhinnie (junction south)	4.8
Kingussie (junction north)	17.3
Aviemore (north junction)	14.9
Tomatin Services	14.2
Inverness Roundabout	17.4
Tore	7.6
Cromarty Firth Bridge	5.6
Alness	5.6
Dornoch Firth Bridge	18.1
Golspie	12.3
Brora Village (south end)	4.8
Helmsdale	12.6
Berriedale	9.1
Dunbeath	6.9
Latheronwheel	2.9
Thrumpster	14.4
Wick	4.8
Reiss	2.9
Keiss	4.9
Auckengill	2.7
Freswick	3.9
John O'Groats	3.1

Total Miles 900

Bed & Breakfast Selection

The following list of B&Bs has been chosen for reasonable prices, comfort and proximity to the cycling route. Most are directly on the route or within a short distance from it. They are not arranged in any order of priority other than route order. Many of those listed are accustomed to having 'End to Enders' staying and they can help and advice when necessary.

You are advised to book in advance, especially during busy holiday periods. Some of the B&Bs listed can provide evening meals, please ask when booking. To obtain further B&Bs refer to the list of T.I.C's in the appendix for the areas you require. Please mention to the B&B that you have this book.

Penzance
Torwood House Hotel, Alexandra Road, Penzance. TR18 4LZ
Tel. 01736 360063
www.torwoodhousehotel.co.uk
email: lyndasowerby@aol.com

Redruth - Near railway station.
Nina & Robert Giles, 42 Clinton Rd, Redruth. TR15 2QE
Tel. 01209 216002
www.lansdowne-guesthouse.co.uk
email: lansdowne@ziplip.com

Launceston
Glencoe Villa, 13, Race Hill, Launceston. PL15 9BB
Tel. 01566 775819/773012
email: keigil.robinson@virgin.net

Crediton - Near railway station.
Mrs. S. Pugsley, Great Park Farm, Crediton. EX17 3PR
Tel. 01363 772050
email: susan.pugsley@virgin.net

Taunton
Brookfield Guest House, 16 Wellington Rd, Taunton.
TA1 4EQ
Tel. 01823 272786
www.brookfieldguesthouse.uk.com
email: info@brookfieldguesthouse.uk.com

Chepstow - Just off roundabout on route.
Valerie Kells, Lower Hardwick, Hardwick Hill,
Chepstow. NP16 5PT
Tel. 01291 620515

Hereford - 5 minutes from Cathedral in centre.
Bouvrie Guest House, 26 Victoria St, Hereford. HR4 0AA
Tel. 01432 266265

Ludlow
The Mount, 61 Gravel Hill, Ludlow, Shropshire. SY8 1QS
Tel. 01584 874084
email: rooms@themountludlow.co.uk

Whitchurch - Just off town centre.
Mrs. D. Clubbe, Pheasant Walk, Terrick Road,
Whitchurch, Shrop. SY13 4JZ
Tel. 01948 667118

Warrington - Near A49 (south)
New House Farm Cottage, Hatton Lane, Hatton,
Warrington. WA4 4BZ
Tel. 01925 730567

Charnock Richard - On route
Hinds Head Hotel, Preston Rd, (A49), Charnock
Richard, Chorley. PR7 5HL
Tel. 01257 791365
email: hazelhindshead@aol.com

Bilsborrow - Nth of Preston on A6
Olde Duncombe House, Garstang Road, Bilsborrow, Preston. PR3 0RE
Tel. 01995 640336
email: oldedunc@aol.com

Kendal - On route
Glenholme Guest House, 43 Milnthorpe Rd, Kendal. LA9 5QG
Tel. 01539 721489
email: glynis@glenholme43.freeserve.co.uk

Shap - On route
Fell House, Main St, Shap, Cumbria. CA10 3NY
Tel. 01931 716343
www.shapaccommodation.co.uk
email: fellhouse@btopenworld.com

Carlisle - Near bus and railway station in centre.
Cornerways Guest House, 107 Warwick Rd, Carlisle. CA1 1EA
Tel. 01228 521733
www.cornerwaysbandb.co.uk
email: info@cornerwaysbandb.co.uk

Lockerbie - Cross motorway bridge on the Dumfries Rd, 400yds on right.
The Elms, Dumfries Rd, Lockerbie. DG11 2EF
Tel. 01576 203898
www.theelms-lockerbie.com
email: enquiries@theelms-lockerbie.com

Crawford - On route
Holmelands Country House, 22 Carlisle Road, Crawford. ML12 6TW
Tel. 01864 502753
www.holmlandscotland.co.uk
email: dan.Davidson@holmlandscotland.co.uk

Airdrie - On B803 at Glenmavis north of Airdrie.
Rowan Lodge, 23 Condorrat Rd, Glenmavis, Airdrie. ML6 0NS
Tel. 01236 753934
www.rowanlodge.com
email: june@rowanlodge.com

Stirling - Near Bannockburn Heritage Centre.
Cambria Guest House, 141 Bannockburn Rd, Stirling.
FK7 0EP
Tel. 01786 814603
www.visitbannockburn.com

Crieff
The Carrick, 57 Burrell St, Crieff. PH7 4DG
 Tel. 01764 656595
www.thecarrick.co.uk

Aberfeldy
Helen Malcolm, Cedar House, 30a, Chapel St,
Aberfeldy. PH15 2AS
Tel. 01887 820779

Kingussie - Approx. 200yds off the A9 (north end),
turning right towards Kingussie then left. A free massage
is available!
The Auld Poor House, Kingussie. PH21 1LS
Tel. 01540 661558
www.yates128.freeserve.co.uk
email: gordon@yates128.freeserve.co.uk

Inverness - In the centre of Inverness near the castle.
Jean & Tony Gatcombe, Ardmuir House, 16 Ness Bank,
Inverness. IV2 4SF
Tel/Fax. 01463 231151
www.ardmuir.com
email: hotel@ardmuir.com

Golspie
Mrs J. Payton, Rhives House, Golspie, KW10 6SD
Tel. 01408 633587
email: jaxx@raxx.freeserve.co.uk

John O'Groats
Sea View Hotel, John O'Groats, Caithness. KW1 4YR
Tel. 01955 611220
www.johnogroats-seaviewhotel.co.uk
email: seaviewhotel@barbox.net

Main Towns/Villages on Route

Lands End   ↓
Penzance   ⬇
Hayle (just off)
Redruth (just off)
Bodmin (just off)
Launceston (just off)
Okehampton
Crediton
Tiverton
Taunton
Bridgwater
Bristol
Chepstow
Monmouth
Hereford
Leominster (just off)
Ludlow
Shrewsbury
Whitchurch
Warrington
Wigan
Preston

Lancaster   ↓
Kendal   ⬇
Penrith
Carlisle
Gretna
Lockerbie (just off)
Lanark
Airdrie
Cumbernauld
Denny
Stirling
Dunblane
Crieff
Aberfeldy
Kingussie (just off)
Aviemore (just off)
Inverness (just off)
Golspie
Brora
Helmsdale
Wick
John O'Groats

Useful Addresses

Lands End - John O'Groats End to End Club
The Customs House
Lands End, Penzance
Cornwall TR19 7AA
Tel. 01736 871501
email: info@landsend-landmark.fsnet.co.uk

Cilla George (home email): cillageorge@aol.com
Advice and information, magazines and special offers for
club members.

National Rail Services. Tel. 08457 484950

Scotrail Ticket Purchases. Tel. 08457 550033

The route described in this book was the one used by the author; it was checked in 2003 and believed to be correct at the time of publication.

Hopefully you have enjoyed this memorable expedition and gained as much pleasure from cycling the route as he did. Please visit Challenge Publications website at: -

www.chall-pub.fsnet.co.uk

A wide selection of guides covering the UK are available including Millennium Cycle Rides in 1066 Country, covering cycling routes in and around East Sussex and containing everything you need to know on a set of laminated cards.

On our website you will find interesting walks around the British Isles, which are picturesque and enjoyable.

Should you wish to comment on this book or give further information to help keep the book updated then please write to the address below or email via the website. An acknowledgement will be given: -

Please write to: -
Challenge Publications
7, Earlsmere Drive,
Ardsley,
Barnsley.
S71 5HH

Lands End to John O'Groats Expedition Diary
Use the following pages to record your experiences, highs
and lows of your walk. You should include the following
on a daily basis.
1. Weather
2. Start/Finish Times
3. Distance Walked
4. Overnight Stay
5. From/To
6. Special Points

Day 1. _____

_____

_____

_____

_____

_____

_____

_____

_____

_____

_____

_____

_____

_____

_____

_____

_____

_____

_____

_____